OCCASIONAL
P A P E R

The Lessons of Mumbai

Angel Rabasa, Robert D. Blackwill,
Peter Chalk, Kim Cragin, C. Christine Fair,
Brian A. Jackson, Brian Michael Jenkins,
Seth G. Jones, Nathaniel Shestak,
Ashley J. Tellis

RAND
CORPORATION

This paper results from the RAND Corporation's continuing program of self-initiated independent research. Support for such research is provided, in part, by donors and by the independent research and development provisions of RAND's contracts for the operation of its U.S. Department of Defense federally funded research and development centers.

Library of Congress Cataloging-in-Publication Data is available for this publication.

978-0-8330-4667-3

Published 2009 by the RAND Corporation
1776 Main Street, P.O. Box 2138, Santa Monica, CA 90407-2138
1200 South Hayes Street, Arlington, VA 22202-5050
4570 Fifth Avenue, Suite 600, Pittsburgh, PA 15213-2665
RAND URL: http://www.rand.org/
To order RAND documents or to obtain additional information, contact
Distribution Services: Telephone: (310) 451-7002;
Fax: (310) 451-6915; Email: order@rand.org

Preface

This study of the Mumbai terrorist attack of November 2008 is part of the RAND Corporation Occasional Papers series. The research for this report was completed in December 2008 and updated as of January 9, 2009. Much of the information available for this necessarily preliminary analysis comes from reporting by the news media, which in such circumstances is often inaccurate, and from information provided by well-placed Indian and U.S. government sources, which sometimes is incomplete. For a thorough, and hopefully accurate reconstruction of events, we must await an official inquiry or government-sponsored independent investigation. With these caveats, this paper

- identifies the operational and tactical features and technical capabilities displayed by the terrorists—the extent to which the means employed in the attack were innovations or built on previous experiences
- evaluates the response of the Indian security forces
- draws out the implications of the incident for India, Pakistan, and the international community
- derives the lessons learned from the attack and the Indian response.

The goal of the study is to develop findings that may be helpful to counterterrorism authorities in India and elsewhere in preparing for or countering future terrorist attacks on urban centers.

This paper results from the RAND Corporation's continuing program of self-initiated independent research. Support for such research is provided, in part, by donors and by the independent research and development provisions of RAND's contracts for the operation of its U.S. Department of Defense federally funded research and development centers.

This research was conducted within the RAND National Security Research Division (NSRD) of the RAND Corporation. NSRD conducts research and analysis for the Office of the Secretary of Defense, the Joint Staff, the Unified Combatant Commands, the defense agencies, the Department of the Navy, the Marine Corps, the U.S. Coast Guard, the U.S. Intelligence Community, allied foreign governments, and foundations.

For more information on the RAND National Security Research Division, contact the Director of Operations, Nurith Berstein. She can be reached by email at Nurith_Berstein@rand.org; by phone at 703-413-1100, extension 5469; or by mail at RAND, 1200 South Hayes Street, Arlington VA 22202-5050. More information about the RAND Corporation is available at www.rand.org.

Contents

Acknowledgments

The authors are thankful to officials and analysts inside and outside the U.S. and Indian governments who shared their insights into the attack and its significance. We are also greatly indebted to the reviewers of this report, Sumit Ganguly, Rabindranath Tagore Chair in Indian Cultures and Civilizations at Indiana University, and William Rosenau, RAND Corporation political scientist, for their suggestions, which greatly improved the quality of the paper. At RAND, Brian Grady, Shivan Sarin, and Phil Kehres provided valuable assistance to the completion of this project. We also thank our editor, Miriam Polon, and production editor, Matthew Byrd, for helping to turn the manuscript into a finished product, and Michael Lostumbo and James Dobbins for their role in quality assurance. Needless to say, any errors and oversights are the responsibility of the authors.

Introduction

The November 26, 2008, terrorist attack in Mumbai, which killed at least 172 people, has been referred to as "India's 9/11." By most measures, it was not the first significant terrorist attack in India. After all, the July 2006 Mumbai commuter train bombings yielded 209 deaths. There was no use of unconventional weapons. And it was not the first time terrorists had landed by sea in Mumbai. Nevertheless, some aspects of this attack were significant, namely, its audacious and ambitious scope, the complexity of the operation, and the diversity of its targets. The prolonged nature of the episode, which went on for 60 hours with the steadily mounting death toll, made it a slow-motion shoot-out and siege that mesmerized the world's news media.

Given previous terrorist attacks in India, it was not difficult to situate the motives for the Mumbai attack in the continuing Islamist terrorist campaign. Evidence suggests that Lashkar-e-Taiba (LeT), a terrorist group based in Pakistan, was responsible for the attack. Pakistan-based terrorists see India as part of the "Crusader-Zionist-Hindu" alliance, and therefore the enemy of Islam. "Muslim" Kashmir ruled by majority "Hindu" India, provides a specific cause, but LeT has always considered the struggle in Kashmir as part of the global struggle, hence the specific selection of Americans and Britons as targets for murder, and the inclusion of the Jewish Chabad center as a principal target. (While most sources allege that the terrorists deliberately targeted Americans and Britons, others, including Jane's, suggest that the shootings at the hotel were as indiscriminate as those at the Chhatrapati Shivaji Terminus). LeT has declared that its objective is not merely liberating Kashmir but breaking up India. More pragmatically, a terrorist attack on India can exacerbate antagonisms between India's Hindu and Muslim communities and provoke Hindu reprisals that, in turn, divide India and facilitate recruiting by Islamist extremists.

Why Mumbai? Mumbai is India's commercial and entertainment center—India's Wall Street, its Hollywood, its Milan. It is a prosperous symbol of modern India. It is also accessible by sea. From the terrorist perspective, the Taj Mahal Palace and Trident-Oberoi Hotels provided ideal venues for killing fields and final bastions. As landmark properties, especially the historic Taj, they were lucrative targets because of the psychological effect of an attack on them. They were filled with people—foreigners and the local elite. The attacks on foreigners guaranteed international media coverage. The message to India was, "Your government cannot protect you. No place is safe." And the international publicity would inevitably result in travel to India being cancelled or postponed with consequent damage to India's economy. The selection of targets—Americans, Britons, and Jews, as well as Indians—suggests that LeT intended the attack to serve a multiplicity of objectives that extended beyond this terrorist group's previous focus on Kashmir and India.

The terrorists' attacks have increased tensions between India and Pakistan, which could have been part of the terrorists' strategic objectives. The prospect of another armed confrontation with India or of India's conducting military attacks on suspected terrorist training bases in Pakistan, will provoke anger and strengthen Pakistani hardliners. That, in turn, will take the pressure off of the terrorists based in Pakistan by forcing a redeployment of Pakistani forces from the frontier tribal areas to the border with India.

LeT's role in the attack raises the issue of Pakistan's own involvement. We do not know for certain whether LeT carried out this operation without the knowledge or approval of Pakistan's army or intelligence services, or whether the attack was instigated or encouraged by sectors of the Pakistani military or intelligence service to change the course of Pakistan's own government. (The implications of these possibilities are discussed elsewhere.)

Terrorist attacks are intended not only to cause fear and alarm but also to inspire terrorist constituencies and attract recruits. By succeeding—and here "success" means humiliating the Indian security services, causing large-scale death and destruction, and garnering global media coverage for days—terrorists hope to attract both Pakistani and Indian recruits to their cause.

The Attack[1]

The Mumbai attack reflected precise planning, detailed reconnaissance, and thorough preparation, both physical and mental. It relied on surprise, creating confusion and overwhelming the ability of the authorities to respond. And it required determined execution by suicide attackers who nonetheless were able to operate effectively over an extended period of time.

Terrorist Reconnaissance and Planning

The complexity of the operation demanded careful preparation. Eyewitness accounts from the Taj Hotel indicate that the terrorists knew their way through hidden doors and back hallways of the hotel. According to another report, the terrorists had a detailed diagram of the hotel's layout.

Indian authorities indicate that in February 2008, a suspected terrorist, arrested in northern India, was found to possess drawings of various sites in Mumbai, some of which were targets in the November 2008 attack. The targets included the Taj Hotel and the Bombay Stock Exchange (which had been a terrorist target in 1993). The apprehended suspect indicated that he had begun his reconnaissance in late 2007. It appears that the planning for the attack itself began in mid-2007. This is consistent with the time line of other large-scale terrorist operations.

To achieve success, the terrorists had to have preplanned routes through the city from the point of their landing to their final objective and had to be very familiar with the terrain they would traverse at night. Information provided by the surviving terrorist in custody indicates that their trainers provided them with maps and CD images of their targets.

Landing by Sea

The Mumbai attackers came by sea, sailing from Karachi on a Pakistani cargo vessel. On November 22 or 23, they hijacked an Indian fishing trawler, murdered its crew except for the

---

[1] This still-preliminary description of the attack is based on media accounts, augmented by private communications with informed American and Indian officials. Jeremy Binnie and Christian Le Miere, "In the Line of Fire: Could Mumbai Happen Again?" *Jane's Intelligence Review,* January 2009, provides a good overview of the sequence of events. An excellent analysis has been compiled by the Intelligence Division of the New York Police Department, which had three officers on the scene in Mumbai. See N.Y.P.D. Intelligence Division, *Mumbai Attack Analysis,* December 4, 2008. In early January, the Indian government released a dossier that included an analysis of the attack and transcripts of cell phone conversations between the terrorists and their handlers during the attack.

captain, and proceeded to Mumbai. They beheaded the captain as they neared their destination. Coming by sea allowed the terrorists to avoid Indian security checkpoints at the frontier or at airports; sailing on an Indian vessel enabled them to avoid arousing the suspicion of the Indian coast guard. The attackers then boarded two small inflatable boats, which they landed at two different points in the southern part of the city.

The Terrorists

We still know very little about the terrorists themselves. The ten attackers are all reported to be Pakistanis in their early 20s. They are believed to have been assisted by an unknown number of locals, including possibly Indian nationals, who helped with reconnaissance and possibly with prepositioned supplies. The one surviving member is a modestly educated (fourth grade) young Pakistani, who reportedly was drifting toward a life of petty crime before being recruited in the jihadist cause. The terrorists spoke Urdu, Hindi, and some English.

The surviving terrorist may know little about his comrades. He reports that members of the team were isolated from one another during most of their training for the mission. According to another unconfirmed report, however, he said that some of the terrorists had come to Mumbai on a reconnaissance mission some time before the attack disguised as students. Some accounts say that at least some members of the attack team may have been on site from up to two months before the attack to conduct reconnaissance and to stockpile ammunition. Official Indian sources, however, indicate that all ten arrived by boat on the night of the attacks.

The surviving terrorist apparently was able to readily identify one of the key leaders of LeT, which would seem to indicate a breach of security if LeT intended to disguise its involvement.

Heavy Firepower

The terrorists came heavily armed. Each carried an AK-56 automatic assault rifle (a Chinese version of the Russian AK-47) with seven magazines of ammunition (30 rounds each). The terrorists also used Heckler & Koch MP5 machine guns but may have taken these from dead or wounded Indian security personnel. The attackers were armed with 9-mm pistols with two clips of ammunition, and they carried hand grenades (8 to 10 grenades each, according to one report). They also had improvised explosive devices (IEDs). Each device reportedly contained the high explosive RDX, ball bearings to create shrapnel, a digital timer, and a 9-volt battery. Five devices were located. Two were left behind in taxis used by the attackers, and three others were left at other locations along their route to detonate later, creating greater confusion. The two devices left in the taxis exploded. The others failed or were rendered safe by Indian bomb squads.

There are varying reports of supplies having been prepositioned. According to one account, Indian commandos discovered a backpack at the Taj Hotel containing seven loaded AK-47 magazines, 400 spare rounds, four hand grenades, and various documents. It is not clear whether the backpack had been carried there by one of the slain attackers.

Tactics

The attack was sequential and highly mobile. Multiple teams attacked several locations at once—combining armed assaults, carjackings, drive-by shootings, prefabricated IEDs, targeted killings (policemen and selected foreigners), building takeovers, and barricade and hostage situations.

While these tactics were a break from the now common suicide bombings associated with jihadist groups, armed assaults have ample precedent in the annals of terrorism, reaching all the way back to the 1972 Lod Airport attack in which three members of the Japanese Red Army opened fire and threw hand grenades at arriving passengers. Barricade and hostage situations were common throughout the 1970s. What was new here was the combination of tactics.

It was a complicated, multipart operation. By dispersing into separate teams and moving from target to target, the terrorists were able to sow confusion and create the impression of a greater number of attackers. The explosive devices that would go off after the terrorists departed heightened the confusion.

The multiple attacks at different locations prevented the authorities from developing an overall assessment of the situation. Media reports consistently overestimated what we now know to be the actual size of the attacking force. The security forces probably had similar difficulties, complicated further by the inevitable erroneous reports that accompany the response to any terrorist event. The small size of the individual attack teams—two to four men—limited their capability in any firefight with security forces. Upon confronting any serious return fire, as they eventually did at the train station, for example, they broke off contact and moved on to another target.

Four Teams

The terrorists divided themselves into four attack teams, one with four men and three with two members each. After landing in Mumbai, one two-man team took a taxi to the Chhatrapati Shivaji Terminus (CRT), Mumbai's main train station, where they took out their weapons and opened fire on commuters. Remarkably, the two were able to roam through the station killing indiscriminately for 90 minutes before better-armed police units arrived, forcing the terrorists to leave the station. Huge numbers of middle-class commuters use this station on a routine basis. While the attacks at the other targets were aimed at killing foreigners, the attack at the train station was aimed at killing ordinary Indian citizens. Killing with apparent impunity seemed intended to instill fear and dread in the minds of the hundreds of thousands of people who use the station for their daily commutes.

The terrorist team then headed to the Cama & Albless Hospital, where they renewed the killing. Escaping again with a police car they had ambushed and hijacked, they headed toward the Trident-Oberoi Hotel, firing along the way. Forced to turn back, they hijacked another vehicle but were finally intercepted by police. In the ensuing gun battle, one terrorist was killed; the second was wounded and captured. This team alone was responsible for a third of the fatalities.

The second team walked to Nariman House, a commercial-residential complex run by the Jewish Chabad Lubavich movement. They threw grenades at a gas station across the street from the complex, opened fire on the building, and then entered the lobby shooting. Taking

13 hostages, five of whom they subsequently murdered, the terrorists prepared for the police assault. This team accounted for eight of the total fatalities.

The third two-man team headed from the landing site to the Trident-Oberoi Hotel, where they began killing people indiscriminately. In a call to the news media, they claimed that seven terrorists were in the building and they demanded that India release all Mujahadeen (Muslim fighters) prisoners in return for the release of the hostages. The siege continued for approximately 17 hours before the terrorists were killed. By the time they died, they had killed 30 people.

The fourth and largest team moved toward the Taj Mahal Palace Hotel. The terrorists briefly entered the Leopold Café, spraying its occupants with automatic weapons fire, killing ten people. Then they moved to the rear entrance of the Taj Hotel only a hundred meters away. They walked through the grounds and ground floor of the hotel, killing along the way, then moved to the upper floors, setting fires and moving constantly in order to confuse and delay government commandos. The siege at the Taj ended 60 hours later, when Indian commandos killed the last of the four terrorists.

The dispersal of the attackers into separate teams indicates an effort to reduce operational risk. Once the attack began, the failure or elimination of any single team would not have put the other teams out of action. The only possible point of failure for the entire attack was while the terrorists were still at sea on their way to Mumbai. This particular pattern of operation—in which the attackers assault and penetrate deep into the target, where they then kill as many as possible—had been seen before in LeT attacks on Indian forces in Kashmir.

Slaughter or Siege?

The attackers' purpose, as indicated by the testimony of the surviving terrorist, was to kill as many people as possible. However, there is some uncertainty that slaughter alone was the sole purpose of the operation's planners. If we compare the 2008 Mumbai attack with the 2006 Mumbai train attack, in which seven bombs killed 209 people, or the 1993 Mumbai attack in which 257 persons died in 13 bomb blasts across the city, it would seem that bombs would have been more effective if body count were the sole criterion.

Indiscriminate bombings, as in the London and Madrid bombings, have been criticized, even by some jihadists, as contrary to an Islamic code of warfare. So it is possible that by relying on shooters, the 2008 attack would appear to be more selective, even though the vast majority of those killed in Mumbai were ordinary Indians gunned down at random. This pretension of selectivity was underscored by the terrorists' purported search for Americans and Britons, by the brutal murders at the Chabad Centre, and by what appear to have been considered decisions to kill certain hostages. It also enabled the attackers to eventually engage the police and soldiers in what their supporters could portray as a heroic last stand.

Security may have been another factor. Based on the pattern of previous terrorist attacks, Indian authorities were focused on truck bombs at hotels. Rail security focused on trying to keep bombs off trains, not armed assailants out of train stations.

An armed assault might also have been more attractive than suicide bombings to the attackers themselves. Once they opened fire, their fate was sealed, but the prolonged nature of the operation enabled them to engage in a sustained slaughter where they could see the results.

Still martyrs in their own minds, they could also think of themselves as being more like warriors than mere button-pushing suicide bombers.

Targets

All the facilities attacked were soft targets. At no point during the attack did the terrorists attempt to overcome armed guards. For the most part, the terrorists attacked unguarded targets, and, even in places where they could expect security forces, their reconnaissance informed them that those forces would be only lightly armed and easily overcome. The main targets included the central train station, the Cama & Albless Hospital, the Leopold Café, the Chabad center, the Trident-Oberoi Hotel, and the Taj Mahal Palace Hotel—the latter target assigned to the only four-man team. Other places attacked along the way were targets of opportunity. Putting aside the drive-by shootings, the train station and the two hotels provided the opportunity for achieving a high body count. The Leopold Café (a famous site) and the hotels were dramatic venues for the attack—providing the "emotional value" sought by terrorists. The massacre at the Chabad center had its own logic. According to transcripts of phone calls between the terrorists and their handlers during the attack, terrorists at the Chabad center were instructed to kill their Jewish hostages in order to "spoil relations between India and Israel."

Communications

The attackers reportedly used cell phones and a satellite phone, both their own and others taken from their victims. They also carried Blackberries. A thoroughly preplanned attack, which Mumbai certainly was, would have required no communications between the terrorist operators and their headquarters. According to a dossier released by Indian authorities, however, the terrorists were in frequent contact with their handlers, presumably based in Pakistan, during the attack. In the transcripts of these phone calls, intercepted by Indian authorities and released in early January, handlers in Pakistan urged the attackers on, exhorting them to kill, reminding them that the prestige of Islam was at stake, and giving them tactical advice that, in part, was gleaned from watching live coverage of the event on television. Despite these exhortations to murder hostages and not to be taken alive, some observers believe—and there are reports that the surviving terrorist thought—that the attackers felt that somehow they were going to get out alive. The terrorists called each other during the siege to discuss their routes of maneuver. They also talked to the news media via cell phones to make demands in return for the release of their hostages. This led Indian authorities to think that they were dealing with a hostage situation, which further confounded their tactical response.

A Strategic Terrorist Culture

The Mumbai attack demonstrates that jihadist organizations based in Pakistan are able to plan and launch ambitious terrorist operations, at least in neighboring countries such as India. Put in the context of previous terrorist attacks in India by Pakistani-based or local jihadist groups, it suggests a continuing, perhaps escalating, terrorist campaign in South Asia. Beyond India, the Mumbai attack reveals a strategic terrorist culture that thoughtfully identified strategic goals and ways to achieve them and that analyzed counterterrorist measures and developed ways to obviate them to produce a 9/11-quality attack. For 60 hours, the terrorists brought a city of 20 million people to a standstill while the world looked on.

The attack put into actual practice LeT's previous rhetoric about making the Kashmir dispute part of the international jihad. In so doing, LeT has emerged, not as a subsidiary of al Qaeda, but as an independent constellation in the global jihad galaxy. Indeed, with al Qaeda central operational capabilities reduced, the Mumbai attack makes LeT a global contender on its own.

The Indian Response

The Indian government's response to the Mumbai attacks highlighted several key weaknesses in the country's general counterterrorism and threat-mitigation structure.

Intelligence Failures. Indian intelligence officials received prior warnings both from their own sources and from the United States that a major attack was probable, but lack of specificity and uncertainty about the threat windows seemed to have prevented specific responses. There appears to have been little coordination between the central security agencies—the Research and Analysis Wing (R&AW) and the Intelligence Bureau (IB)—and the local police in Bombay. Although the former are known to have intercepted "chatter" about a possible LeT seaborne attack on Mumbai, it is not clear whether the Mumbai police (or the Indian coast guard) received the information. At any rate, they did not act upon it. This issue highlights the universal problem of rapidly disseminating covert intelligence for actionable purposes.[1]

Gaps in Coastal Surveillance. The attacks highlighted India's inability to effectively monitor its coastline—a condition that is common to many littoral states in both the developing and the developed world. Although R&AW had information (apparently secured from intercepts) about a possible terrorist landing by sea, whatever measures were taken proved insufficient to monitor maritime traffic in and around Mumbai. This failure would seem to reflect the coast guard's shortage of equipment for coastal surveillance: fewer than 100 boats for more than 5,000 miles of shoreline and minimal aviation assets. Although the central government has set aside funds for the purchase of 26 additional vessels to patrol the country's coastal states, Maharashtra State (of which Mumbai is the capital) refused them on the grounds that it lacked the funds necessary for maintenance.[2]

Inadequate "Target Hardening." The metal detectors at the CRT were of questionable reliability, and, although the Railway Protection Force (RPF) officers were armed, their weapons were relatively antiquated and in short supply (one for every two officers). The attack on the railway terminus also underscored the limitations of the RPF in terms of concerted counterterrorism: Although the force has the ability to fend off common criminals, it is completely lacking in training to deal with a well-orchestrated terrorist attack.[3]

---

[1] Sumit Ganguly, "Delhi's Three Fatal Flaws," *Newsweek*, December 8, 2008; Ajai Sahni, "Mumbai: The Uneducable Indian," *South Asia Intelligence Review*, Vol. 7, No. 21, 2008. It should be noted that these problems are not unique to India and, indeed, have been identified as a major factor in the United States' own intelligence failures in connection with the 9/11 attacks.

[2] Sunita Parikh, "Mumbai Attacks Highlight Shortcomings in Indian Terror Response," *The Beacon*, December 5, 2008; Padma Rao Sundarji, "How India Fumbled Response to Mumbai Attack," *McClatchy Newspapers*, December 3, 2008.

[3] Sahni, "Mumbai: The Uneducable Indian," p. 3; Damien McElroy, "Mumbai Attacks: Foreign Governments Criticise India's Response," *The Daily Telegraph* (UK), November 28, 2008; Sundarji, "How India Fumbled Response to Mumbai Attack."

Incomplete Execution of Response Protocols. Although local police contingents (including the Anti-Terrorism Squad, or ATS) responded relatively quickly, they lacked both the training to set up appropriate command posts and dragnets for sealing off the attack sites. In particular, they failed to cordon off the attack sites along a wide perimeter to contain the terrorists. Because the attacks were at multiple locations, police did not have the ability to cordon the area. It was the terrorists' purpose, based on previous experience, not to give the police a containable event—a key lesson learned from what the terrorists did.

Response Timing Problems. Local contingents of the army arrived at the scene of the attacks at 02:50 hours, a full five hours after the first shots had been fired.[4] The first "special response" team, the Marine Commandos (Marcos), arrived a little later, but the unit was pulled out before engaging any of the terrorists. It was not until 08:50 hours that the elite National Security Guard (NSG, or "Black Cat Commandos," which are modeled on the pattern of the British SAS and German GSG-9) arrived. Initial search-and-rescue operations were mounted some 30 minutes later, and it is only at that point that the terrorists could seriously be considered engaged.[5]

The slow response of the NSG is especially noteworthy given its mandate to act as the country's premier rapid-reaction force. This underscores two main organizational and logistical problems. First, the unit is headquartered south of Delhi and lacks bases anywhere else in the country;[6] second, the NSG has no aircraft of its own and cannot count on dedicated access to Indian Air Force aircraft in an emergency. The only plane that was available to transport the 200 commandos to Mumbai was a Russian IL-76 transport carrier; however, it was in Chandigarh, which is 165 miles south of Delhi. The pilot had to be awakened, a crew assembled, and the plane fueled. The aircraft did not reach Delhi until 02:00 hours (five hours after the attacks began and most of the killing had been done) and took roughly 3.5 hours to reach Mumbai (compared to just two hours for a commercial jet). According to various counterterrorism experts, any rapid-reaction force must reach the scene of a terrorist incident no later than 30–60 minutes after it has commenced. In Mumbai, nearly 10 hours elapsed.[7]

Inadequate Counterterrorism Training and Equipment for the Local Police. To effectively manage a terrorist incident, first responders need to have appropriate equipment and training to neutralize or at least contain the terrorists. However, the Mumbai attacks graphically illustrated how ill prepared the Maharashtra police were to handle a major terrorist incident. Many police officers remained passive, seemingly because they were outgunned by the terrorists. The bulletproof vests that were available could not withstand AK-47 or AK-56 rounds (two batches had failed tests in 2001 and 2004, and the head of the ATS, Chief Karkare, died after bullets

---

4   This, however, may be less of a response timing problem than an issue of political decisionmaking.

5   Sahni, "Mumbai: The Uneducable Indian," p. 3; Parikh, "Mumbai Attacks Highlight Shortcomings in Indian Terror Response"; "Major Terrorism Incident: The Mumbai Assault," *Jane's Terrorism and Insurgency Centre (JTIC) Special Report*, December 1, 2008, pp. 7–8.

6   Following criticism of the time it took the NSG to arrive in Mumbai, the government of India has announced that additional base units will be set up in Mumbai, Kolkata, Chennai, Bangalore, and Hyderabad. Delhi has also pledged to create a nationwide agency tasked with counterterrorism duties; to establish a coastal command to secure the country's 7,500 km of shoreline; to fill vacancies in intelligence agencies; to upgrade technology; to establish new dedicated counterterrorism commando forces; to build counterinsurgency and counterterrorism training schools; and to strengthen laws relating to the prevention, investigation, and punishment of terrorist acts. "After Mumbai, India Unveils Anti-Terror Measures," Reuters, December 11, 2008.

7   Sahni, "Mumbai: The Uneducable Indian," p. 3; Sundarji, "How India Fumbled Response to Mumbai Attack."

penetrated the vest he was wearing). Many officers had only been issued 5-mm-thick plastic protectors that were suitable for riot control but not for engaging terrorists. Helmets were of World War II vintage and not designed for modern combat, and most of the responding detachments involved in the incidents were carrying .303 bolt-action rifles of the sort used by the British Army in the 1950s.[8]

Limitations of Municipal Fire and Emergency Services. Firemen were slow to respond. They failed to coordinate their actions with both the local police and national paramilitary forces and suffered from inadequate equipment. These limitations underscore the poor quality of India's municipal services even in a major, bustling, economically vibrant city such as Mumbai.[9]

Flawed Hostage-Rescue Plan. In several respects, the NSG hostage rescue plans for the Taj Mahal and Trident-Oberoi Hotels suffered from serious defects. The unit's senior command failed to set up an operational command center to coordinate the mission, and the storm teams went in "blind" with no understanding of the basic layout of either of the two buildings. Both hotels were designated "clear" when terrorists were still alive; room-to-room sweeps were hampered by insufficient intelligence on the numbers of hostages being held and the profile of the militants involved; and the possibility for a surprise raid under cover of darkness was effectively negated by the absence of suitable equipment, such as night-vision goggles and thermal imaging systems.[10]

Poor Strategic Communications and Information Management. Throughout the crisis, the central government and security forces failed to project an image of control, with the words "chaos" and "paralysis" used repeatedly to describe events as they unfolded.[11] So badly did officials handle communications that an unprecedented public interest lawsuit has been filed against the government charging that it failed to discharge its constitutional duty to protect the country's citizenry and uphold their right to life.[12] More seriously, breaches of basic information security protocols provided the terrorists with vital operational intelligence. Major criticism was directed at a cabinet minister on the first day of the crisis, after he announced that 200 NSG commandos were to be deployed in the area in two hours. Not only did this alert the terrorists as to when a hostage rescue mission might occur, it also effectively confirmed that no forward operating units had yet been mobilized.[13]

Since the attack, the Indian government has announced a number of reforms aimed at addressing these various shortcomings. On December 11, 2008, India's Home Minister, P. Chidambaram, announced several efforts to improve India's domestic security, including the creation of a Coastal Command to secure 4,650 miles of shoreline, establishment of 20

---

[8] Sundarji, "How India Fumbled Response to Mumbai Attack"; Parikh, "Mumbai Attacks Highlight Shortcomings in Indian Terror Response"; Jeremy Page, "Outgunned Mumbai Police Hampered by First World War Weapons," *TimesOnline*, December 3, 2008.

[9] Again, it should be noted that these problems are not unique to India. They were also identified in post-9/11 inquiries as limiting the effectiveness of the U.S. government's response to the September 11 attacks.

[10] Sahni, "Mumbai: The Uneducable Indian," p. 4; McElroy, "Mumbai Attacks: Foreign Governments Criticise India's Response."

[11] Sahni, "Mumbai: The Uneducable Indian," p. 3.

[12] Somini Sengupta, "Mumbai Attacks Politicize Long-Isolated Elite," *The New York Times*, December 7, 2008.

[13] McElroy, "Mumbai Attacks: Foreign Governments Criticize India's Response."

counter-terror schools and standing regional commando units, creation of a national agency to investigate suspected terror activity, and strengthening of anti-terror laws.[14]

India's parliament has taken steps to make some of these reforms a reality. On December 17, India's lower house (Lok Sabha) approved new anti-terror legislation; it was approved by the upper house (Rajya Sabha) the next day. The new Unlawful Activities (Prevention) Act provides new powers to the security services, including the ability to hold suspects for six months without charges. It also makes provisions to establish a National Investigative Agency that will be responsible for investigating terrorism and gathering and processing intelligence. Some of these provisions (such as lengthy detentions without charge) have drawn domestic criticism.[15]

Following the 1999 incursion by Pakistani paramilitary forces in the Kargil-Dras sectors of Kashmir, the Indian government vowed to institute reforms intended to make future incursions less likely. Many of these changes were proposed in the Kargil Review Commission Report. Since then, few of those enhancements have been implemented. Thus, it remains to be seen whether India will follow through on efforts to improve domestic security and over what time horizon.[16]

On January 5, 2009, India, unsatisfied with Pakistan's response so far, issued a 69-page dossier detailing the linkages between the Mumbai attackers and Pakistan. The dossier was given to Pakistan to satisfy Pakistan's demand for evidence of Pakistani involvement. India hopes that by mounting a comprehensive diplomatic offensive, it can persuade the international community to act more forcefully to influence Pakistan to shut down LeT, Jaish-e-Mohammad (JM), and other militant groups operating in and from Pakistan. Following the release of the dossier, Indian officials asserted that the attack "must have had the support of some official agencies in Pakistan."[17]

---

[14] Rama Lakshmi, "Indian Official Unveils Plan to Strengthen Security," *Washington Post*, December 11, 2008.

[15] "UAPA Retains Most of POTA's Stringent Provisions," Times of India, December 17, 2008. http://timesofindia .indiatimes.com/India/UAPA_retains_most_of_POTAs_stringent_provisions/articleshow/3847843.cms.

[16] The recommendations of the Kargil Review Committee can be accessed at http://mod.nic.in/newadditions/annexb .pdf.

[17] A text of the dossier is available at http://www.hindu.com/nic/dossier.htm. Also see Siddharth Varadarajan, "After Evidence Dossier, Direct Accusation Against Pakistan Strikes Discordant Note," *The Hindu*, January 8, 2009.

Implications

The LeT attacks on Mumbai have serious implications for India, Pakistan, the United States and, in some measure, the international community. While many of the implications for these four actors remain the same irrespective of the degree of autonomy with which LeT executed these attacks, as detailed below, other implications change dramatically if we assume some degree of state sponsorship.

India

The attack has a number of external and internal implications for India. Both are considered here. With respect to India's relationship with Pakistan, Indians are convinced that LeT is sponsored by Pakistani government entities, as recent official statements attest. India will therefore respond in a way that holds the government of Pakistan responsible. The connections between LeT and Pakistan's Directorate for Inter-Services Intelligence (ISI) are well known, as are LeT's various camps and offices in Pakistan.[1] Moreover, India has been victimized by a host of militant groups based in and supported by Pakistan for decades.[2] With the possible exception of the militant groups associated with Jamaat-Islami, the so-called Kashmir *tanzeems* have been raised, nurtured, assisted, and trained by the ISI. As such, these groups are not strictly nonstate actors but rather extensions of the state intelligence apparatus, albeit with some degree of plausible deniability. After becoming an overt nuclear power, Pakistan has become emboldened to prosecute conflict at the lower end of the spectrum, confident that nuclear weapons minimize the likelihood of an Indian military reaction.

In the wake of nuclearization, substate conflict expanded dramatically. In 2001, a RAND analysis of the aforementioned Kargil crisis found that the Pakistani operation was enabled by the protective nuclear umbrella ensuring that India's conventional response would be constrained. Similarly, groups that were previously limited to the Kashmir theater expanded into the Indian hinterland following the 1998 nuclear tests. Notable attacks included the 2000 LeT attack on the Red Fort, the 2001 JM attack on the Indian parliament, the 2006 LeT Mumbai subway attack, and numerous other attacks by LeT or JM throughout India. In addition, in

---

[1] See, for example, the discussion in Husain Haqqani, *Pakistan: Between Mosque and Military,* Washington D.C.: Carnegie Endowment for International Peace, 2005; Muhammad Amir Rana, *A to Z of Jehadi Organizations in Pakistan,* trans. Saba Ansari, Lahore, Pakistan: Mashal Books, 2004; Amir Mir, *True Face of the Jehadis,* Lahore, Pakistan: Mashal Books, 2004.

[2] Alexander Evan, "The Kashmir Insurgency: As Bad As It Gets," *Small Wars & Insurgencies,* Vol. 11, No. 1, Spring 2000, pp. 69–81; Haqqani, *Pakistan: Between Mosque and Military.*

2000, LeT introduced the *fidayeen* (high-risk commando) operation in Kashmir and has since used it throughout India.[3]

For these reasons, India has not (and likely will not) acquiesce to the prevalent Pakistani position that this attack, like others before it, is the handiwork of nonstate actors that the state does not control. This attack has refocused Indian policymakers' attention on overhauling their internal security mechanisms even as it strengthens the Indian military's interest in developing the means to punish Pakistan for such attacks and to deter future ones.[4]

Despite some Indian interest in military options, there do not appear to be at present any military operations that can have strategic-level effects without significant risk of military response from Pakistan. While air or land strikes across the line of control (LoC) could satisfy an Indian polity exhausted with Pakistan-based terror, strikes across the LoC would only be able to target camps in Azad Kashmir. Such strikes would not cripple the wider infrastructure of terrorism in Pakistan, given that LeT and other militant groups have relocated to the Federally Administered Tribal Areas and have assets in nearly every province of Pakistan. Striking across the LOC or the international border will be risky and may precipitate a wider crisis given Pakistan's ability to respond conventionally and unconventionally.

While India understands the costs of military action, from its point of view there are also costs to *not* responding. Since 2001, India has suffered a number of militant attacks that have involved in varying degrees Pakistan-based and indigenous militants. Indian officials believe that this terrorism is official Pakistani policy. Given India's beliefs about the origins of the various attacks perpetrated on its soil, India exhibited exceeding restraint in the aftermath of the 2006 LeT attack on Mumbai's subway system. Pakistan has likely concluded from the events since the December 2001 attack on the Indian parliament complex and prior, that India is unable or unwilling to mount a serious effort to punish and deter Pakistan for these attacks. Accordingly, from India's vantage point, to not respond would signal a lack of Indian resolve or capability. The pressure to act is likely to remain even if Pakistan takes some form of action against specific LeT activists. Indian proponents of military action believe that some sort of military response is required to ensure that Pakistan (or at least those elements of its military and intelligence leadership that are supportive of the activities of groups like LeT) understands that terrorism in India is no longer a cost-free option.[5]

For the foreseeable future, India is likely to remain a target of Pakistan-based terrorism. This is due, among other things, to India's inability (and indeed that of the international community) to compel Pakistan to dismantle the terrorist infrastructure comprehensively; to Pakistan's inherent incapacities to do so even if it had the will; and to the expanding participation of

---

[3]   See Ashley J. Tellis, C. Christine Fair, and Jamison Jo Medby, *Limited Conflicts Under the Nuclear Umbrella—Indian and Pakistani Lessons from the Kargil Crisis,* Santa Monica: RAND, 2001; S. Paul Kapur, "India and Pakistan's Unstable Peace: Why Nuclear South Asia Is Not Like Cold War Europe," *International Security,* Vol. 30, No. 2, Fall 2005, pp. 138–139; Ashley J. Tellis, *Pakistan and the War on Terror: Conflicted Goals, Compromised Performance,* Washington D.C.: Carnegie Endowment for International Peace, 2008; Walter C. Ladwig III, "A Cold Start for Hot Wars? The Indian Army's New Limited War Doctrine," *International Security,* Vol. 32, No. 3, Winter 2007–2008, pp. 158–190.

[4]   This has principally taken the form of an emergent limited war doctrine called Cold Start.

[5]   See, for example, "India's Military Options," *The Hindustan Times,* December 5, 2008; "Pak Making No Serious Attempt to Dismantle Terror Camps: Antony," *Times of India,* January 8, 2008; "India Shouldn't Rule Out Military Option: Former Army Chief," *Thaindian News,* December 17, 2008.

Indians in Islamist violence with varying degrees of assistance from Pakistan and Bangladesh.[6] This attack, building upon a recent history of dozens of attacks in India, also underscores India's dire need to redress its numerous deficiencies in its internal security arrangements.

There are several likely areas of much-needed attention, many of which have been highlighted elsewhere in this paper. There is considerable variation in the size, competence, and capabilities of India's various state police forces. However, few would disagree that India has too few competent police for its citizenry overall, especially given that at any one time it is combating several active insurgencies in addition to fending off terrorist attacks launched from inside and outside the country. Ajai Sahni, a well-known terrorism analyst in Delhi, has long criticized India's low police-to-population ratio of about 125 per 100,000. (Because policing is under the control of the individual states, state police forces vary in end-strength.) This figure is nearly half the U.N.-recommended ratio for peacetime policing, much less a country with numerous active insurgencies.[7]

As the footage of the most recent terrorist outrage demonstrates, Indian police are outgunned by their foes. They are also generally poorly trained and lack the ability to collect, store, and analyze forensic evidence in accordance with international standards. In addition to its generally decrepit state of policing, India—like many other countries—has difficulty moving intelligence from its central intelligence agencies to state-level counterparts. As the militants' frequent reliance upon the sea route attests, India remains vulnerable to such attacks. This underscores the urgent need for greater coastal security.

Since most external terrorist groups require some local collaborators for the success of their missions, all likely targets within India ought to undertake a quiet but urgent review of their own personnel to minimize the probability of terrorists securing insider access or information.

Pakistan

It is in many ways too early to assess the full range of ramifications for Pakistan. They will depend in good measure upon the evolving U.S. and Indian responses, Pakistan's own domestic actions against the country's myriad militant groups, and the response of the international community. The consequences for Pakistan are also considerably different depending on the extent of the linkages between the ISI and LeT in general and the conduct of this operation in particular. India contends that LeT required the participation of Pakistan's intelligence agencies to execute the attack. Notably, Prime Minister Singh suggested, "There is enough evidence to show that, given the sophistication and military precision of the attack, it must have had the support of some official agencies in Pakistan."[8]

Indian and American officials by and large believe that Pakistan's civilian government does not control the military's (or ISI's) policies toward militant groups operating in and from

---

6   Lisa Curtis, "After Mumbai: Time to Strengthen U.S.–India Counterterrorism Cooperation," Heritage Foundation Backgrounder #2217, December 9, 2008. For some treatment of the communal violence issue, see Paul R. Brass, *The Production of Hindu-Muslim Violence in Contemporary India*, Seattle, Wash.: University of Washington Press, 2003; Ashutosh Varshney, *Ethnic Conflict and Civic Life*, New Haven, Conn.: Yale University Press, 2002.

7   Ajai Sahni, "The Uneducable Indian" (op-ed), *Outlook* (Delhi), December 1, 2008.

8   Somini Sengupta, "Dossier Gives Details of Mumbai Attacks," *The New York Times*, January 6, 2009.

Pakistan. Most analysts of Pakistan now believe that Pakistan's best hope is to slowly civilianize and incrementally exert civilian control over the military and intelligence agencies, but few are optimistic that this can or will occur. The challenge for the United States, India, and the international community is how to selectively put pressure on the military and intelligence agencies in the near term without destabilizing Pakistan's fragile civilian government. No doubt, the Pakistan security establishment understands this calculus and therefore discounts the likelihood of significant reprisals. If so, Pakistan is very likely to take the minimal steps needed to defuse the present crisis while still retaining a capacity to use militants in the future.

If LeT operated with some degree of complicity from the military and intelligence agencies, the Mumbai attack offers a number of disturbing implications. First, it suggests that attacking India with the aim of weakening it remains the ambition of at least some key elements in the Pakistani security establishment. Second, it would have served the purpose of derailing the government's policies of pursuing rapprochement with India and fighting extremists in the tribal areas, as well as the efforts of the United States to intervene in the Pakistani Army's doctrine and training. Thus, the attack may have been calibrated to engender an Indian military response and to provide some respite from unpopular operations along the Afghanistan border. Finally and most importantly for the United States, the persistence of ties between Pakistani intelligence and military entities and groups such as LeT suggests that Pakistan's intelligence and military establishment may not be a reliable security partner of the United States.

If LeT undertook the attack without military or ISI sanction, LeT will have joined the ranks of the other militant groups that were once ISI proxies but are now increasingly hostile to the Pakistani state in some measure. For example, after 2002, Jaish-e-Mohammad split into two factions, one of which favored targeting the state and its Western allies and one that favored continued cooperation with the Pakistani state. Pakistan may now be a victim of the groups it created.

While it is doubtful that LeT has turned its back on its erstwhile handlers, it is not impossible.[9] LeT has significant external sources of funding and is less dependent upon the ISI than in the past. LeT may have judged that the benefits of working with the ISI and abiding by its guidelines are not worth the constraints on its operations. No doubt the Mumbai attack will allow LeT to expand its recruitment and fundraising. Moreover, since LeT has been cooperating more closely with al Qaeda in Afghanistan, it may have decided to target the "Zionist-Hindu-Crusader" alliance about which it has long ranted in its various literature and public addresses.

---

[9] K. Alan Kronstadt of the Congressional Research Service has recently written of ISI-LeT ties (*Terrorist Attacks in Mumbai, India, and Implications for U.S. Interests*, Washington D.C.: Congressional Research Service, December 2008, p. 5),

> . . . an unnamed, but ostensibly high-ranking Indian official claimed that his government has "clear and incontrovertible proof" that the November Mumbai attack was planned by the LeT with training and other support from the ISI. U.S. officials have to date been more circumspect . . . but many are reported to believe that the LeT's recent growth in strength and reach has come only with active assistance from ISI elements, either active or "retired." In mid-2008, U.S. intelligence officials apparently concluded that ISI elements were involved in a July car bombing of India's Embassy in Kabul, Afghanistan.

Ashley Tellis has also written recently that LeT has "subterranean links with the ISI." See Ashley J. Tellis, "Terrorists Attacking Mumbai Have Global Agenda," *Yale Global*, December 8, 2008.

Judging from President Zardari's statements and the delayed response of the Pakistani government to the crisis, Pakistan's civilian government is either unwilling to comprehensively shut down LeT and its front organization, Jamaat ul-Dawa (JuD), or, more likely, is seriously constrained from doing so by the military and intelligence agencies. As late as December 17, 2008, President Zardari denied the credibility of the evidence that the surviving attacker, Ajmal Qasab, is a Pakistani despite the admission of Qasab's own father.[10] On January 7, 2009, National Security Advisor Mahmood Durrani was fired because he intimated during an interview with CNN that the attackers had roots in Pakistan. The prime minister's spokesman, Imran Gardaizi, explained that he was dismissed because "he gave media interviews on national security issues without consulting the prime minister."[11]

Despite the denials espoused by the civilian government, it has undertaken a number of belated steps against LeT. Pakistan was extremely reluctant to ban JuD, but promised to do so after the United Nations Security Council proscribed the group, a move that required China's backing.[12] (Only a year before, China had declined to back a similar move.) On December 11, 2008, Pakistan finally put JuD's leader Hafiz Muhammad Saeed under house arrest and sealed nine JuD offices in Lahore, Karachi, Hyderabad, Peshawar, and Mansehra linked to the Mumbai attack, including the Jamia Masjid Qudsia, the main JuD office in Lahore. It is unclear whether the police have taken any action to shut down JuD headquarters in Muridke.[13] (Saeed was previously put under house arrest only to be released.) Media reports suggest that there is lackadaisical security enforcing his house arrest; one newspaper report noted that it was more akin to a "forced vacation."[14] Finally, on December 13, 2008, Pakistan banned JuD, a move decried by some of Pakistan's politicians.[15] However, reports have already surfaced suggesting that JuD has again reorganized under yet a new guise. [16]

Pakistan's sluggish response to LeT may have several explanations, all of which could be at play in some measure. Parts of the Pakistani security establishment likely still view the organization as a valuable asset in some measure. Alternatively, the state may have been reticent to take on LeT at this time because it cannot do so competently. Finally, even if the civilian government (or its political leadership) is convinced that these groups threaten Pakistan and the region, they do not control the security apparatus and have limited ability to suppress the groups without further undermining their own hold in power.

---

[10] BBC World Service, "Zardari Distances Pakistan from Mumbai Attack," December 17, 2008.

[11] "Pakistan Fires National Security Adviser," Associated Press, January 7, 2009; "Pakistan's National Security Advisor Fired After Mumbai Disclosure," VOA News, January 7, 2009.

[12] On December 10, 2008, the United Nations Security Council placed financial sanctions on four members of LeT (Muhammad Saeed, whom the UN names as the group's leader; Zaki-ur-Rehman Lakhvi, described as LeT's chief of operations; Haji Muhammad Ashraf, its finance chief; and Mahmoud Mohammad Ahmed Bahaziq, described as a financier for the group). The four face an assets freeze, a travel ban, and an arms embargo. In addition, the Security Council amended its 2005 blacklisting of LeT to include the charitable foundation JuD after Pakistan banned LeT. Pakistani President Asif Ali Zardari said that he would ban JuD if given conclusive evidence of its links to the Mumbai attack. Jay Solomon, "U.N. Security Council Sanctions Lashkar Members," *The Wall Street Journal,* December 10, 2008.

[13] Nirupama Subramanian, "Crackdown on Jamat-ud-Dawah," *The Hindu,* December 12, 2008.

[14] Richard A. Oppel and Salman Masood, "With House Arrest Pakistan Curbs, Lightly, a Leader Tied to Mumbai Attackers," *The New York Times,* December 12, 2008.

[15] Sridhar Krishnaswami, "Pakistan Banned Jamat-ud-Dawah for Its Own Interest, Says US," *The Hindustan Times,* December 13, 2008; "Jud Ban Illegal, Says Imran Khan," *Times Now,* December 24, 2008.

[16] "Banned JuD Back Under New Name: Menon," *Indian Express,* January 2, 2008.

The United States

The Mumbai attack attests to ongoing shortcomings—if not outright failure—in the United States' efforts to manage its various security interests in Pakistan and the region. As is well known, in the early phase of the war on terror, the United States tended to focus its efforts on securing Pakistan's cooperation in pursuing al Qaeda. In part because the United States believed the Taliban had been defeated, it did not pressure Pakistan to cooperate against the Taliban until 2007, although interest in doing so percolated across the U.S. government in 2006. This renewed interest was due in large measure to the Taliban resurgence in 2005, which to a large extent was facilitated by the sanctuary that the Taliban and other extremists enjoyed in Pakistan. Washington applied only episodic pressure on Pakistan to eliminate the groups operating in Kashmir, of which LeT was one. According to one well-placed advisor to the Bush administration, even placing LeT on the foreign terrorist organization list was a challenge because the administration was concerned about the reaction of the Pakistani army.

In an effort to secure Pakistan's cooperation in the global war on terrorism, the United States focused its energies and its resources on the Pakistan military. Between fiscal years 2002 and 2008, the United States spent more than $11.2 billion presumably to further these goals.[17] In return, the United States has secured access to Pakistani soil for logistical supply as well as access to naval and air bases for the conduct of Operation Enduring Freedom. Pakistan has also deployed significant numbers of military and paramilitary troops along the border with Afghanistan, where it has engaged in operations with varying success against selected militants considered to be a threat to the state.

In the main, U.S. policies have not secured a comprehensive commitment from Pakistan to eliminate militants based in Pakistan. Taliban leaders and warlords—Jallaluddin Haqqani, Gulbuddin Hekmatyar, and Baitullah Meshud, among others—remain free to operate from Pakistani soil with impunity, and many believe that the Pakistani military and the ISI actively support them.[18] Equally alarming, LeT has been targeting U.S. and NATO forces in Afghanistan's Kunar and Nuristan provinces at least since 2007. This is in addition to the ongoing operations against India by a number of groups based in Pakistan.

The International Community

With the Mumbai attack, LeT demonstrated that it has the ability and the will to internationalize its targets. LeT now has now assumed a larger role in the larger jihadi landscape. Like some of the other militant groups in Pakistan, LeT is believed to have considerable reach into Pakistani diaspora populations, raising a number of concerns for countries with Pakistani expatriate communities. More than ever, India and her partners need to forge more robust counterterrorism and law enforcement links. For the policy-relevant future, Pakistan will remain a destination where individuals radicalized abroad can go to obtain training from militant groups. Thus, containing the threat posed by militants in Pakistan is an international challenge with few mechanisms to support it. The Indian government successfully pre-

---

[17] K. Alan Kronstadt, "Pakistan-US Relations," *CRS Report for Congress*, Washington D.C.: Congressional Research Service, August 2008.

[18] Seth Jones, "Pakistan's Dangerous Game," *Survival*, Vol. 49, No. 1, 2007, pp. 15–32.

vailed upon the United Nations to take action against LeT and key leaders. While the United Nations may have little impact upon LeT's ability to act, China's vote was necessary to secure this vote. As China has long been seen as Pakistan's most reliable partner, this vote may have some impact in Islamabad.

Key Judgments

India will continue to face a serious jihadi terrorist threat from Pakistan-based terrorist groups for the foreseeable future. However, India lacks military options that have strategic-level effects without a significant risk of a military response by Pakistan. Neither Indian nor U.S. policy is likely to be able to reduce that threat significantly in the short to medium term. Most likely, the threat will continue to grow. Other extremists in India inevitably will find inspiration and instruction from the Mumbai attack.

Safe havens continue to be key enablers for terrorist groups. Safe havens allow terrorist leaders to recruit, select, and train their operators and make it easier for terrorists to plan and execute complex operations, such as the Mumbai attack. Therefore, at the strategic level, the Mumbai attack underscores the imperative of addressing the transnational sources of Islamist terrorism in India. How to do this is an extraordinarily difficult question that will require the reassessment of basic assumptions concerning policy toward Pakistan by members of the international community.

The focus on Pakistan in this case should not obscure the likelihood that the attackers had local assistance or that other recent terrorist attacks in India appear to have been carried wholly or partially by Indian nationals. Local radicalization is a major goal of the terrorists and will remain a major political and social challenge for India.

The masterminds of the Mumbai terrorist attack displayed sophisticated strategic thinking in their choice of targets and tactics. The attack appears to have been designed to achieve an array of political objectives. This indicates a level of strategic thought—a strategic culture—that makes this terrorist foe particularly dangerous.

Given that the terrorists seek to maximize the psychological impact of the attacks, we can expect that future attacks will aim at both large-scale casualties and symbolic targets. The jihadists have stated, and the Mumbai attack demonstrates, the determination of the terrorists to seek high body counts, go after iconic targets, and cause economic damage.

The terrorists will continue to demonstrate tactical adaptability, which will make it difficult to plan security measures around past threats or a few threat scenarios. Terrorists innovate. They designed the Mumbai attack to do what authorities were not expecting. There were no truck bombs or people attempting to smuggle bombs onto trains, as in previous attacks.

Since attacks against high-profile soft targets are relatively easy and cheap to mount, such institutions will remain targets of future attacks. The protection of those targets presents particularly difficult challenges. Many of India's older symbolic buildings were not built with security considerations in mind or are in exposed locations.

Iconic institutions that are likely to be potential targets of terrorist attack must work with local police and intelligence agencies to receive timely alerts about possible threats. They must work with local municipalities and police to curtail open vehicular access to their premises and must consider putting in place screening barriers at some distance from their physical premises where this is possible. They must also develop preplanned response strategies, in coordination with local law enforcement, to the wide variety of possible threats that can be reasonably envisaged.

One of the most important lessons of this attack is the continuing importance of an earlier operational form: the firearms assault. While the counterterrorism world has been focused almost exclusively on explosives, this attack demonstrates that firearms assault, while not as deadly as mass-casualty bombings, can be an effective tactic in creating prolonged chaos in an urban setting

Intelligence failure, inadequate counterterrorist training and equipment of local police, delays in the response of NSG commandos, flawed hostage-rescue plans, and poor strategic communications and information management all contributed to a less-than-optimal response. These gaps suggest the need for improved counterterrorist coordination between national-level and local security agencies and for strengthened counterterrorist capabilities on the part of first responders. Unless India can improve the quality and functioning of its entire internal security apparatus, it will remain acutely vulnerable to further terrorist penetration and attacks.

Chronology of the Attack

November 26, 2008 (all times are local)

21:20 Gunfire outside the Hotel Oberoi at Nariman Point in south Mumbai.

21:20 Terrorists run into Nariman House, where they take control of the Chabad Lubavich center.

21:30 Gunfire outside the Leopold Café at Colaba in south Mumbai, about 100 meters behind the Taj Mahal Palace Hotel.

21:40 Gunfire near the Bade Miyan Café (behind the Taj Hotel in south Mumbai).

21:45 Terrorists enter Taj Hotel lobby and fire indiscriminately.

21:45 Gunfire inside the Chhatrapati Shivaji Terminus (CST), Mumbai's central train station. There are ten fatalities there.

22:30 Gunfire at the Municipal Corporation of Greater Mumbai headquarters gate 2, opposite the CST.

22:35 Gunfire at Gokuldas Hospital, near the CST.

22:40 Gunfire at the Cama & Albless Hospital, near the CST.

22:50 Gunfire at the Metro Theatre (Metro Cinema Junction).

23:00 Explosion in a taxi in Vile Parle in north Mumbai. (This is one of the IEDs left behind in the taxi.)

23:00 Explosion in a taxi in Mazgaon—probably the second IED left behind.

23:10 Two explosions at Napean Sea Road in south Mumbai.

23:30 Explosion at Dhobi Talao.

November 27, 2008

00:30 Gunfire after a police van was hijacked at Dhobi Talao.

01:00 Immense blast in the Taj Hotel, possibly caused by two grenades.

02:00 Army arrives at the Taj Hotel.

03:00 Large fire breaks out at the Taj Hotel.

09:15 Army arrives at Oberoi Hotel, storm hotel.

09:15 Security forces engage in first attempt to retake the Taj Hotel.

10:30 Security forces engage in room-to-room searches at the Taj Hotel.

17:30 NSG forces arrive at Nariman House. Helicopters begin surveillance.

November 28, 2008

07:30   NSG forces storm Nariman House.

11:00   Hostage siege ends at the Hotel Oberoi, hostages released.

11:00   NSG forces report that they have cleared the new section of the Taj Hotel.

13:00   Indian security forces report 30 people dead in one Taj Hotel hall.

18:00   Operations reported to have ceased at Nariman House. However, NDTV reports that one floor still has not been cleared.

19:45   All NSG forces emerge from Nariman House, stating that no one was found alive.

November 29, 2008

04:30   Gunfire and explosions heard at the Taj Hotel.

07:30   Fire breaks out on the lower floors of the Taj Hotel.

08:50   Taj Hotel hostage siege declared over, according to Indian police.

Bibliography

"After Mumbai, India Unveils Anti-Terror Measures," Reuters, December 11, 2008.

"Banned JuD Back Under New Name: Menon," *Indian Express*, January 2, 2008. As of January 8, 2009:
http://www.indianexpress.com/news/banned-jud-back-under-new-name-menon/405594/

BBC World Service, "Zardari Distances Pakistan from Mumbai Attack," December 17, 2008. Interview online. As of January 8, 2009:
http://www.bbc.co.uk/worldservice/news/2008/12/081217_zardari_nh_sl.shtml

Binnie, Jeremy, and Christian Le Miere, "In the Line of Fire: Could Mumbai Happen Again?" *Jane's Intelligence Review,* January 2009.

Brass, Paul R., *The Production of Hindu-Muslim Violence in Contemporary India*, Seattle, Wash.: University of Washington Press, 2003.

Curtis, Lisa, "After Mumbai: Time to Strengthen U.S.–India Counterterrorism Cooperation," Heritage Foundation Backgrounder #2217, December 9, 2008. As of December 10, 2008:
http://www.heritage.org/Research/AsiaandthePacific/bg2217.cfm#_ftn8

Evan, Alexander, "The Kashmir Insurgency: As Bad As It Gets," *Small Wars & Insurgencies*, Vol. 11, No. 1, Spring 2000.

Ganguly, Sumit, "Delhi's Three Fatal Flaws," *Newsweek*, December 8, 2008. As of January 14, 2009:
http://www.newsweek.com/id/171318/page/1

Haqqani, Husain, *Pakistan: Between Mosque and Military*, Washington D.C.: Carnegie Endowment for International Peace, 2005.

"India's Military Options," *The Hindustan Times,* December 5, 2008, As of January 14, 2009:
http://www.hindustantimes.com/news/specials/popup/30_12_D_MTR11.pdf

Jones, Seth, "Pakistan's Dangerous Game," *Survival,* Vol. 49, No. 1, 2007.

"JuD Ban Illegal, Says Imran Khan," *Times Now*, December 24, 2008. As of January 8, 2009:
http://timesnow.tv/NewsDtls.aspx?NewsID=24409

Kapur, S. Paul, "India and Pakistan's Unstable Peace: Why Nuclear South Asia Is Not Like Cold War Europe," *International Security*, Vol. 30, No. 2, Fall 2005, pp. 138–139.

Krishnaswami, Sridhar, "Pakistan Banned Jamat-ud-Dawah for Its Own Interest, Says US," *The Hindustan Times*, December 13, 2008. As of January 8, 2009:
http://www.hindustantimes.com/StoryPage/StoryPage.aspx?sectionName=&id=0ba46c92-e702-40bc-80b7-ace8928c8a9e&&Headline='Pakistan+banned+Jamat-ud-Dawah+for+its+interest

Kronstadt, K. Alan, "Pakistan–U.S. Relations," CRS Report for Congress, Washington D.C.: Congressional Research Service, August 2008. As of January 8, 2009:
http://www.fas.org/sgp/crs/row/RL33498.pdf

———, *Terrorist Attacks in Mumbai, India, and Implications for U.S. Interests*, CRS Report for Congress, Washington D.C.: Congressional Research Service, December 19, 2008. As of January 14, 2009:
http://www.spearheadresearch.org/Pages/Documents/R40087%20(2).pdf

Ladwig III, Walter C., "A Cold Start for Hot Wars? The Indian Army's New Limited War Doctrine," *International Security*, Vol. 32, No. 3, Winter 2007–2008.

Lakshmi, Rama, "Indian Official Unveils Plan to Strengthen Security," *Washington Post,* December 11, 2008. As of January 8, 2009:
http://www.washingtonpost.com/wp-dyn/content/article/2008/12/11/AR2008121100942.html

"Major Terrorism Incident: The Mumbai Assault," *Jane's Terrorism and Insurgency Centre (JTIC) Special Report*, December 1, 2008.

McElroy, Damien, "Mumbai Attacks: Foreign Governments Criticise India's Response," *The Daily Telegraph* (UK), November 28, 2008. As of January 14, 2008:
http://www.telegraph.co.uk/news/worldnews/asia/india/3533279/Mumbai-attacks-foreign-governments-criticise-indias-response.html

Mir, Amir, *True Face of the Jehadis*, Lahore, Pakistan: Mashal Books, 2004.

New York Police Department Intelligence Division, *Mumbai Attack Analysis,* December 4, 2008.

Oppel, Richard A., and Salman Masood, "With House Arrest Pakistan Curbs, Lightly, a Leader Tied to Mumbai Attackers," *The New York Times*, December 12, 2008. As of January 8, 2009:
http://www.nytimes.com/2008/12/13/world/asia/13pstan.html?_r=3

Page, Jeremy, "Outgunned Mumbai Police Hampered by First World War Weapons," *TimesOnline*, December 3, 2008. As of December 10, 2008:
http://www.timesonline.co.uk/tol/news/world/asia/article5276283.ece

"Pak Making No Serious Attempt to Dismantle Terror Camps: Antony," *Times of India,* January 8, 2008. As of January 14, 2009:
http://timesofindia.indiatimes.com/India/Pak_making_no_serious_attempt_to_dismantle_terror_camps_Antony/articleshow/3948353.cms

"Pakistan Fires National Security Adviser," Associated Press, January 7, 2009. As of January 8, 2009:
http://www.google.com/hostednews/ap/article/ALeqM5giM6p8lktZjdppbdN6WYC1NpBuSAD95IFNO80

"Pakistan's National Security Advisor Fired After Mumbai Disclosure," VOA News, January 7, 2009. As of January 8, 2009:
http://voanews.com/english/2009-01-07-voa38.cfm

Parikh, Sunita, "Mumbai Attacks Highlight Shortcomings in Indian Terror Response," *The Beacon*, December 5, 2008. As of December 10, 2008:
http://www.stlbeacon.org/index2.php?option=com_content&task=view&id=5258&pop=1&page=0&Itemid=83

Rana, Muhammad Amir, *A to Z of Jehadi Organizations in Pakistan*, trans. Saba Ansari, Lahore, Pakistan: Mashal Books, 2004.

Sahni, Ajai, "Mumbai: The Uneducable Indian," *South Asia Intelligence Review*, Vol. 7, No. 21, 2008. As of January 14, 2009:
http://satp.org/satporgtp/sair/Archives/7_21.htm#assessment1

————, "The Uneducable Indian" (op-ed), *Outlook* (Delhi), December 1, 2008.

Sengupta, Somini, "Dossier Gives Details of Mumbai Attacks," *The New York Times*, January 6, 2009. As of January 8, 2009:
http://www.nytimes.com/2009/01/07/world/asia/07india.html?em

————, "Mumbai Attacks Politicize Long-Isolated Elite," *The New York Times*, December 6, 2008. As of January 8, 2009:
http://www.nytimes.com/2008/12/07/world/asia/07india.html?fta=y

Solomon, Jay, "U.N. Security Council Sanctions Lashkar Members," *The Wall Street Journal*, December 10, 2008. As of December 11, 2008:
http://online.wsj.com/article/SB122895332614496341.html?mod=googlenews_wsj

Subramanian, Nirupama, "Crackdown on Jamat-ud-Dawah," *The Hindu*, December 12, 2008. As of December 11, 2008:
http://www.hindu.com/2008/12/12/stories/2008121250010100.htm

Sundarji, Padma Rao, "How India Fumbled Response to Mumbai Attack," McClatchy Newspapers, December 3, 2008. As of December 2008:
http://news.yahoo.com/s/mcclatchy/20081204/wl_mcclatchy/3115227

Tellis, Ashley J., *Pakistan and the War on Terror: Conflicted Goals, Compromised Performance*, Washington D.C.: Carnegie Endowment for International Peace, 2008.

————, "Terrorists Attacking Mumbai Have Global Agenda," *Yale Global*, December 8, 2008. As of January 14, 2009:
http://yaleglobal.yale.edu/display.article?id=11695

Tellis, Ashley J., C. Christine Fair, and Jamison Jo Medby, *Limited Conflicts Under the Nuclear Umbrella—Indian and Pakistani Lessons from the Kargil Crisis*, Santa Monica, Calif.: RAND Corporation, MR-1450-USCA, 2002. As of January 14, 2009:
http://www.rand.org/pubs/monograph_reports/MR1450/

"UAPA Retains Most of POTA's Stringent Provisions," *Times of India,* December 17, 2008. As of January 14, 2009:
http://timesofindia.indiatimes.com/India/UAPA_retains_most_of_POTAs_stringent_provisions/articleshow/3847843.cms

Varadarajan, Siddharth, "After Evidence Dossier, Direct Accusation Against Pakistan Strikes Discordant Note," *The Hindu,* January 8, 2009. As of January 14, 2009:
http://www.hindu.com/2009/01/08/stories/2009010859721000.htm

Varshney, Ashutosh, *Ethnic Conflict and Civic Life*, New Haven, Conn.: Yale University Press, 2002.